DEDICATION

This book is dedicated to all the ambitious and organized people out there who love to celebrate Halloween.

Your are my inspiration for producing books and I'm honored to be a part of keeping all your Halloween planning and notes all in one place.

This journal notebook will help you record your details for the month of October and any events that you plan for Halloween.

Thoughtfully put together with these sections to record: October Calendar, Halloween Checklist, Place For Photos, Halloween & Fall Bucket List, Costume Planner, Classroom Party Planner, Decoration Planner, Halloween Crafts & Planner, Halloween Recipes, Budget Tracker, Journal & Memories Pages and much more.

HOW TO USE THIS BOOK

The purpose of this book is to keep all of your lists and notes all in one place. It will help keep you organized.

This Halloween Planner Journal will allow you to accurately document .

Here are examples of the prompts for you to fill in and write about yourself in this book:

1. October Calendar - Blank, undated October calendar so you can see your plans and specials days in overview.
2. Halloween Checklist - Overview detailed checklists for everything including: Costumes, Decorations, Trick or Treating, Halloween Parties, Classroom Parties.
3. Halloween Planner Page - Write Events, Crafts To Create, Treats To Make, Costume Choices, Movies To Watch, Books To Read & Your Traditions.
4. Place For Photos - Place for you to glue or tape your pictures.
5. Halloween & Fall Bucket List - Write everything you want to do this Halloween and Fall.
6. Costume Planner - For writing which costume is chosen, clothing pieces & accessories (Enough for 8 people).
7. Classroom Party Planner - Record Teacher Name, Grade, Party Date & Time, Items Needed, Quantity, Parent Volunteers To Help.
8. Decoration Planner - Record Indoor Decorations, Outdoor Decorations, Trick or Treat Entrance Decorations & Shopping List.
9. Halloween Crafts & Planner - Write the Project Name, Description, Instructions Source, Materials Needed, Project Steps & Shopping List.
10. Party Planner, Guest Checklist, Party Food, Treats & Drink Checklist - Record Party Theme, Party For, Adults Invited, Children Invited, Invitations, Decorations, Entertainment: Games & Activities, Party Details, Menu & Favors, Notes. Guests information, Party Food, Treats & Drink Items, Cost & Notes.
11. Halloween Recipes - For Writing the recipes you want to make.
12. Budget Tracker - Write Item, Budgeted, Actual Cost & Difference.
13. Journal & Memories Pages - Plenty of blank lined, ruled pages to write everything about your day, any important details you want to remember, etc.

OCTOBER

Sunday	Monday	Tuesday	Wednesday	Thursday	Friday	Saturday

SUPER FUN PLANS   SPECIAL DAYS

Date:

[JOURNAL]

Date:

JOURNAL

Date:

Master To-Do List

[HALLOWEEN Checklist]

Costumes

- ○ Have kids decide on costumes.
- ○ Make a list of costume pieces and accessories to buy.
- ○ Purchase, order, or make fire-retardant costumes.
- ○ Try on costumes to make sure they fit and aren't a tripping hazard.
- ○ Have sweatshirts, jacket, etc. in case of cold or rainy weather.
- ○ Practice Halloween makeup.

Decorations

- ○ Decorate your home's interior.
- ○ Carve pumpkins.
- ○ Decorate the outside of your home.
- ○ Create a welcoming entrance for trick-or-treaters.
- ○
- ○
- ○
- ○

Trick-or-Treating

- ○ Mark trick-or-treat night on the calendar.
- ○ Establish a route, schedule, and chaperones for the evening.
- ○ Purchase Halloween candy and bowl to hold the treats.
- ○ Go over the safety rules.
- ○ Purchase glow-in-the dark items or reflective tape.
- ○ Purchase trick-or-treat bag or bucket.
- ○ Check flashlight or lantern batteries.
- ○ Take pictures of your kids in their costumes.
- ○ Have fun trick-or-treating!
- ○
- ○
- ○

Halloween Parties

- ○ Create a guest list.
- ○ Set a date and time.
- ○ Purchase or make invitations.
- ○ Set a theme and plan decorations & favors.
- ○ Plan party games and activities.
- ○ Plan the menu.
- ○ Buy party supplies.
- ○ Plan the party timeline.
- ○ Prepare favors, crafts, games, etc.
- ○ Decorate and setup for the party.
- ○ Prepare and set out the party foods.
- ○ Enjoy time with your spooky guest!.
- ○
- ○
- ○

Classroom Parties

- ○ Ask the teacher for input and guidelines.
- ○ Choose the snacks and drinks.
- ○ Pick crafts and activities.
- ○ Make a list of supplies you'll need.
- ○ Create a sign up sheet for the party.
- ○ Ask for volunteers to help during the party.
- ○
- ○
- ○
- ○
- ○

[FALL BUCKET List]

This is going to be the best fall ever!

[COSTUME Planner]

Name:

Costume	Clothing Pieces	Accessories
	○	○
	○	○
	○	○
	○	○
	○	○

Name:

Costume	Clothing Pieces	Accessories
	○	○
	○	○
	○	○
	○	○
	○	○

Name:

Costume	Clothing Pieces	Accessories
	○	○
	○	○
	○	○
	○	○
	○	○

Name:

Costume	Clothing Pieces	Accessories
	○	○
	○	○
	○	○
	○	○
	○	○

[COSTUME Planner]

Name:

Costume	Clothing Pieces	Accessories
	○	○
	○	○
	○	○
	○	○
	○	○

Name:

Costume	Clothing Pieces	Accessories
	○	○
	○	○
	○	○
	○	○
	○	○

Name:

Costume	Clothing Pieces	Accessories
	○	○
	○	○
	○	○
	○	○
	○	○

Name:

Costume	Clothing Pieces	Accessories
	○	○
	○	○
	○	○
	○	○
	○	○

[COSTUME *Planner*]

Name:

Costume	Clothing Pieces	Accessories
	○	○
	○	○
	○	○
	○	○
	○	○

Name:

Costume	Clothing Pieces	Accessories
	○	○
	○	○
	○	○
	○	○
	○	○

Name:

Costume	Clothing Pieces	Accessories
	○	○
	○	○
	○	○
	○	○
	○	○

Name:

Costume	Clothing Pieces	Accessories
	○	○
	○	○
	○	○
	○	○
	○	○

[CLASS Party]

Teacher Name	Grade	Classroom	Party Date & Time

Items Needed	Quantity	Name

Parent Volunteers to Help With:	Name

QUESTIONS? PLEASE CONTACT:

[CLASS Party]

Teacher Name	Grade	Classroom	Party Date & Time

Items Needed	Quantity	Name

Parent Volunteers to Help With:	Name

QUESTIONS? PLEASE CONTACT:

[DECORATION Planner]

Indoor Decorations

Outdoor Decorations

Trick-or-Treat Entrance

Shopping List

Decorations

Costumes & Accessories

Trick-or-Treating

Pumpkin Carving

Groceries

Parties & Paper Goods

[HALLOWEEN Crafts]

Project

Project Name:

Description:

Instructions Source:

Materials Needed

- [ ]
- [ ]
- [ ]
- [ ]
- [ ]
- [ ]
- [ ]
- [ ]
- [ ]
- [ ]
- [ ]
- [ ]

Project Steps

Shopping List

○
○
○
○
○
○
○
○
○
○
○
○
○
○
○
○
○
○
○
○

NOTES

[HALLOWEEN Crafts]

Project

Project Name:

Description:

Instructions Source:

Materials Needed

Project Steps

Shopping List

NOTES

Project

Project Name:

Description:

Instructions Source:

Materials Needed

- [ ]
- [ ]
- [ ]
- [ ]
- [ ]
- [ ]
- [ ]
- [ ]
- [ ]
- [ ]
- [ ]
- [ ]

Project Steps

Shopping List

- ○
- ○
- ○
- ○
- ○
- ○
- ○
- ○
- ○
- ○
- ○
- ○
- ○
- ○
- ○
- ○
- ○
- ○
- ○

NOTES

[HALLOWEEN Planner]

Fun Times

Date	Event

OUR COSTUMES

Craft to Create

Movies to Watch

Treats to Make

Books to Read

TRADITIONS

[HALLOWEEN Planner]

Fun Times

Date	Event

OUR COSTUMES

Craft to Create

Movies to Watch

Treats to Make

Books to Read

TRADITIONS

[HALLOWEEN Planner]

Fun Times

Date	Event

Craft to Create

Treats to Make

OUR COSTUMES

Movies to Watch

Books to Read

TRADITIONS

[PARTY *Planner*]

Party for:

Party Theme:

Adults Invited: Children Invited:

Party Details	
Location:	
Address:	
Date:	
Time:	
Phone:	
Email/Website:	

Invitations

Invitations Needed:	Mail by:
○ Ordered	○ Making
○	○
○	○

Decorations

- ○
- ○
- ○
- ○
- ○

Menu

- ○
- ○
- ○
- ○
- ○

Entertainment/Games/Activities

○	○
○	○
○	○
○	○
○	○

Favors

- ○
- ○
- ○
- ○
- ○

NOTES

[PARTY *Planner*]

Party for:

Party Theme:

Adults Invited: Children Invited:

Invitations

Invitations Needed: Mail by:

○ Ordered ○ Making

Party Details

Location:

Address:

Date:

Time:

Phone:

Email/Website:

Decorations

Menu

Entertainment/Games/Activities

Favors

NOTES

[HALLOWEEN Recipes]

Recipe for:

Servings: Prep Time: Cook Time:

Ingredients

Directions

NOTES

[HALLOWEEN Recipes]

Recipe for:

Servings: **Prep Time:** **Cook Time:**

Ingredients

Directions

NOTES

HALLOWEEN Recipes

Recipe for:

Servings:　　　　　　　　　Prep Time:　　　　　　　　　Cook Time:

Ingredients

Directions

NOTES

[TRICK-OR- Treat]

| Trick-or-Treat Night | Starting Location | Time |

Trick-or-Treaters and Accompanying Adults

The Best House of the Night:

The Best Costume we Saw:

The Route

The Funniest Thing That Happened:

My Candy Totals: How Many?

To Do List

- ○
- ○
- ○
- ○
- ○

TRICK-OR- Treat

Trick-or-Treat Night | Starting Location | Time

Trick-or-Treaters and Accompanying Adults

The Route

To Do List

The Best House of the Night:

The Best Costume we Saw:

The Funniest Thing That Happened:

My Candy Totals: | How Many?

TRICK-OR-Treat

Trick-or-Treat Night	Starting Location	Time

Trick-or-Treaters and Accompanying Adults

The Route

To Do List

- ○
- ○
- ○
- ○
- ○

The Best House of the Night:

The Best Costume we Saw:

The Funniest Thing That Happened:

My Candy Totals:	How Many?

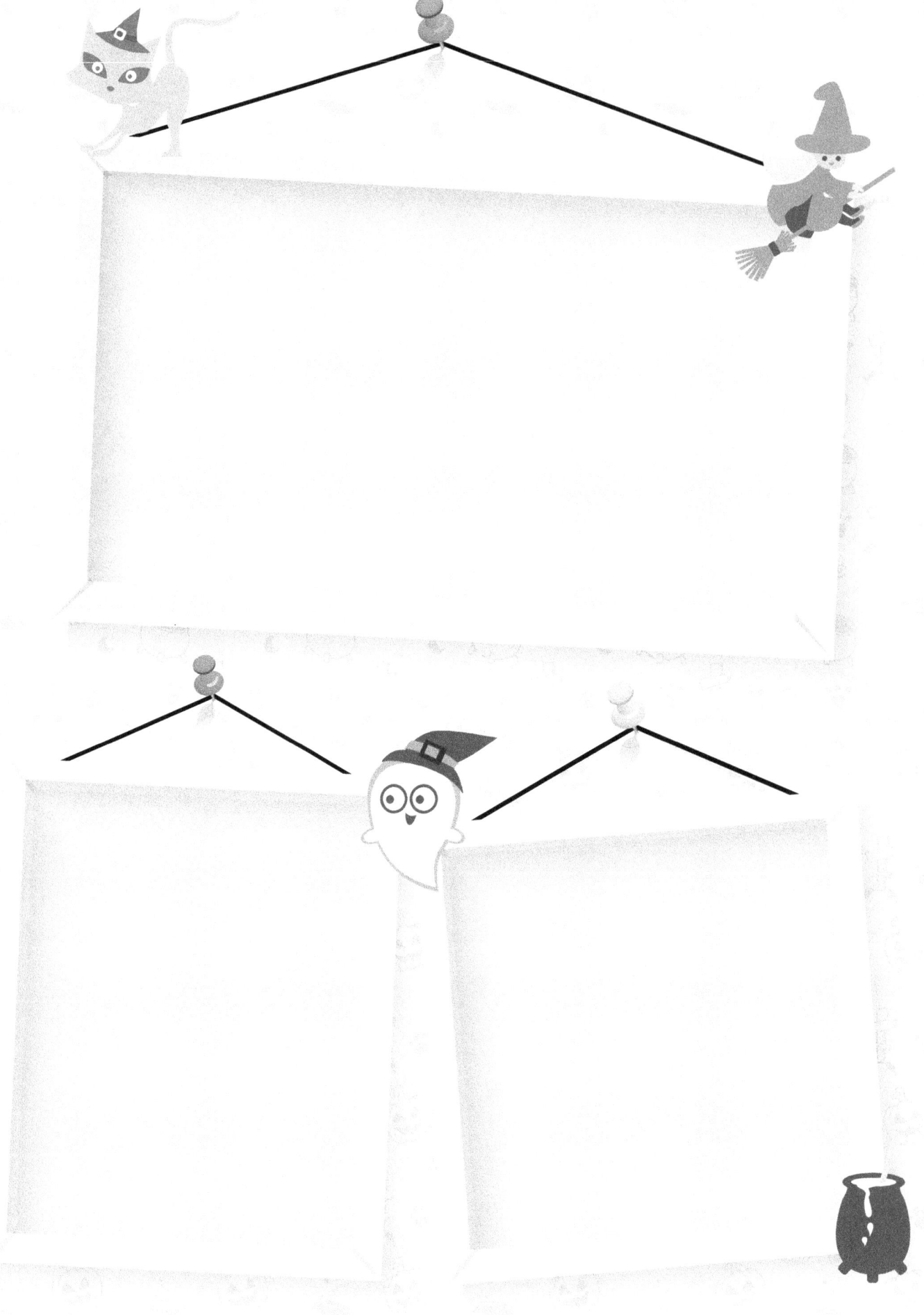

[THIS WEEK'S To-Do's]

Sunday	Monday	Tuesday	Wednesday	Thursday	Friday	Saturday

TOP 3 GOALS
1.
2.
3.

Call/Email/Text

Things to Do

Errands

Notes

[THIS WEEK'S To-Do's]

Sunday	Monday	Tuesday	Wednesday	Thursday	Friday	Saturday

TOP 3 GOALS
1.
2.
3.

Call/Email/Text

Things to Do

Errands

Notes

[THIS WEEK'S To-Do's]

Sunday	Monday	Tuesday	Wednesday	Thursday	Friday	Saturday
☐	☐	☐	☐	☐	☐	☐

TOP 3 GOALS

1.
2.
3.

Things to Do

☐
☐
☐
☐
☐
☐
☐
☐
☐
☐

Call/Email/Text

Errands

Notes

THEME Ideas

Theme Idea
Decoration
Drops
Candy Treats
Food & Drink
Activities
Notes

Theme Idea
Decoration
Drops
Candy Treats
Food & Drink
Activities
Notes

Theme Idea
Decoration
Drops
Candy Treats
Food & Drink
Activities
Notes

Theme Idea
Decoration
Drops
Candy Treats
Food & Drink
Activities
Notes

THEME Ideas

Theme Idea
Decoration
Drops
Candy Treats
Food & Drink
Activities
Notes

Theme Idea
Decoration
Drops
Candy Treats
Food & Drink
Activities
Notes

Theme Idea
Decoration
Drops
Candy Treats
Food & Drink
Activities
Notes

Theme Idea
Decoration
Drops
Candy Treats
Food & Drink
Activities
Notes

GUESTS CHECK List

Name:

Attended with:

Email:

Contact Number:

Mailing Address

Party Favor:

Thank You Card:

Name:

Attended with:

Email:

Contact Number:

Mailing Address

Party Favor:

Thank You Card:

Name:

Attended with:

Email:

Contact Number:

Mailing Address

Party Favor:

Thank You Card:

Name:

Attended with:

Email:

Contact Number:

Mailing Address

Party Favor:

Thank You Card:

Name:

Attended with:

Email:

Contact Number:

Mailing Address

Party Favor:

Thank You Card:

Name:

Attended with:

Email:

Contact Number:

Mailing Address

Party Favor:

Thank You Card:

[GUESTS CHECK List]

Name:	Name:
Attended with:	Attended with:
Email:	Email:
Contact Number:	Contact Number:
Mailing Address	Mailing Address
Party Favor:	Party Favor:
Thank You Card:	Thank You Card:
Name:	Name:
Attended with:	Attended with:
Email:	Email:
Contact Number:	Contact Number:
Mailing Address	Mailing Address
Party Favor:	Party Favor:
Thank You Card:	Thank You Card:
Name:	Name:
Attended with:	Attended with:
Email:	Email:
Contact Number:	Contact Number:
Mailing Address	Mailing Address
Party Favor:	Party Favor:
Thank You Card:	Thank You Card:

GUESTS CHECK List

Name:	Name:
Attended with:	Attended with:
Email:	Email:
Contact Number:	Contact Number:
Mailing Address	Mailing Address
Party Favor:	Party Favor:
Thank You Card:	Thank You Card:
Name:	Name:
Attended with:	Attended with:
Email:	Email:
Contact Number:	Contact Number:
Mailing Address	Mailing Address
Party Favor:	Party Favor:
Thank You Card:	Thank You Card:
Name:	Name:
Attended with:	Attended with:
Email:	Email:
Contact Number:	Contact Number:
Mailing Address	Mailing Address
Party Favor:	Party Favor:
Thank You Card:	Thank You Card:

GUESTS CHECK List

Name:	Name:
Attended with:	Attended with:
Email:	Email:
Contact Number:	Contact Number:
Mailing Address	Mailing Address
Party Favor:	Party Favor:
Thank You Card:	Thank You Card:
Name:	Name:
Attended with:	Attended with:
Email:	Email:
Contact Number:	Contact Number:
Mailing Address	Mailing Address
Party Favor:	Party Favor:
Thank You Card:	Thank You Card:
Name:	Name:
Attended with:	Attended with:
Email:	Email:
Contact Number:	Contact Number:
Mailing Address	Mailing Address
Party Favor:	Party Favor:
Thank You Card:	Thank You Card:

[PARTY FOOD CHECK List]

ITEM	COST	NOTES

[PARTY DRINK CHECK List]

ITEM	COST	NOTES

[PARTY TREATS CHECK *List*]

ITEM	COST	NOTES

PARTY DECORATIONS CHECK List

ITEM	COST	NOTES

PARTY COSTUMES CHECK List

ITEM	COST	NOTES

[PARTY SHOPPING List]

ITEM	COST	NOTES

PARTY SHOPPING List

ITEM	COST	NOTES

DRAW YOUR CRAFT IDEA

Name:

Time to Make:

Color Ideas:

How to Make:

Tools	Materials	Others
☐	☐	☐
☐	☐	☐
☐	☐	☐
☐	☐	☐
☐	☐	☐
☐	☐	☐
☐	☐	☐

[CRAFTS *Planner*]

DRAW YOUR CRAFT IDEA

Name:

Time to Make:

Color Ideas:

How to Make:

Tools	Materials	Others
☐	☐	☐
☐	☐	☐
☐	☐	☐
☐	☐	☐
☐	☐	☐
☐	☐	☐
☐	☐	☐
☐	☐	☐

[CRAFTS Planner]

DRAW YOUR CRAFT IDEA

Name:

Time to Make:

Color Ideas:

How to Make:

Tools	Materials	Others
☐	☐	☐
☐	☐	☐
☐	☐	☐
☐	☐	☐
☐	☐	☐
☐	☐	☐
☐	☐	☐
☐	☐	☐

Date:

HALLOWEEN BUCKET List

BUDGET Tracker

Item	Budgeted	Actual	Difference
Total			

CHORE Chart

ITEM	M	T	W	TH	F	S	S
1.							
2.							
3.							
4.							
5.							
6.							
7.							
8.							
9.							
10.							
11.							
12.							

WEEKLY TASK

○
○
○
○

My Goal This Week	My Reward	Total Chores Completed

[JOURNAL]

Date:

JOURNAL

Date:

JOURNAL

Date:

MEMORIES

Date:

[MEMORIES]

Date:

Date:

www.ingramcontent.com/pod-product-compliance
Lightning Source LLC
Chambersburg PA
CBHW081235080526
44587CB00022B/3952